USA TODAY. TEEN WISE GUIDES
A GANNETT COMPANY

LIFESTYLE CHOICES

VOLUNTEERING

SMARTS

How to Find Opportunities, Create a Positive Experience, and More

SANDY DONOVAN

TWENTY-FIRST CENTURY BOOKS / MINNEAPOLIS

Twenty-First Century Books
A division of Lerner Publishing Group, Inc.
241 First Avenue North
Minneapolis, MN 55401 U.S.A.

Website address: www.lernerbooks.com

Library of Congress Cataloging-in-Publication Data

Donovan, Sandra, 1967–
    Volunteering smarts : how to find opportunities, create a positive experience, and more / by Sandra Donovan.
       p. cm. — (USA TODAY teen wise guides: lifestyle choices)
    Includes bibliographical references and index.
    ISBN 978-0-7613-7021-5 (lib. bdg. : alk. paper)
    1. Voluntarism—United States—Juvenile literature. 2. Voluntarism—Juvenile literature. 3. Volunteers—United States—Juvenile literature. 4. Volunteers—Juvenile literature. 5. Teenage volunteers in social service—United States—Juvenile literature. 6. Teenage volunteers in social service—Juvenile literature. I. Title.
    HN90.V64D66 2013
    302'.14—dc23   2011044265

The images in this book are used with the permission of: © John Giustina/Stone/Getty Images, p. 4; © Jim West/Alamy, pp. 5, 58; © Stephen Miller/USA TODAY, p. 6 (left); © KidStock/Blend Images/Getty Images, pp. 6-7; © Kevin Dodge/CORBIS, p. 10; © imagebroker.net/SuperStock, p. 11; AP Photo/Charles Dharapak, p. 12; © Ariel Skelley/Blend Images/Getty Images, p. 13; © pumkinpie/Alamy, p. 14; © Simon Jarratt/CORBIS, p. 15; © Jamie Grill/Iconica/Getty Images, p. 16; © Eileen Blass/USA TODAY, pp. 17, 41, 51; © Chuck Haupt/American Red Cross , p. 18 (left); © Ken Bennett/USA TODAY, pp. 18-19; © Truth Leem/USA TODAY, p. 20; © Inti St Clair/Digital Vision/Getty Images, p. 21; AP Photo/The Forum, Michael Vosburg, p. 22; © Marilyn Angel Wynn/Nativestock/Getty Images, p. 24 (top); © iStockphoto.com/Tibor Nagy, p. 24 (bottom); © Todd Strand/Independent Picture Service, pp. 27, 43, 52; © Tim Pannell/CORBIS, p. 28; © Samantha Appleton/White House/Handout/CNP/Corbis, p. 29; © Hill Street Studios/Blend Images/Getty Images, p. 30 (left); © Robert Hanashiro/USA TODAY, pp. 30-31; © age fotostock /SuperStock, p. 33; © Erin Brethauer/USA TODAY, p. 34; © MBI/Alamy, p. 36; © C. Devan/CORBIS, p. 39; © H. Darr Beiser/USA TODAY, p. 44 (left); © Joe Raedle/Getty Images, pp. 44-45; © Jeff Greenberg/Alamy, p. 48; © Anne Ackermann/Digital Vision/Getty Images, p. 50; © The Washington Post/Getty Images, p. 53; © Samantha Sin/AFP/Getty Images, p. 55; AP Photo/Steve Cannon, p. 56. Front cover: © Heidi Orcino Photography/Workbook Stock/Getty Images.

Main body text set in Conduit ITC Std 11/15
Typeface provided by International Typeface Corp

Manufactured in the United States of America
1 – PP – 7/15/12

CONTENTS

INTRODUCTION
WHY *Volunteer?*

Alyssa's bummed out. "Every day on my way to school, I pass this same group of homeless people gathered under that bridge," she tells her friend Amir. "And now that winter's coming, I notice them even more, shivering in thin shirts. I think about all the warm clothes we have, and it makes me feel guilty."

"I know what you mean," Amir says. "I worry about problems like that too. But sometimes it feels hard to make a difference when you think about all the people and causes that need help."

Then Amir pauses for a moment, thinking. "You know," he begins again, "This kind of reminds me of something. You know how I've always wanted be a veterinarian?"

"Um, yeah," Alyssa says, wondering what this could have to do with helping homeless people.

"Well, I got freaked out when I heard that becoming a vet is one of the hardest career goals out there. I heard there are at least twenty

Volunteering at a place like a soup kitchen is a great way to help out the homeless and other underprivileged people in your community.

applicants for every open vet job. But then I decided that instead of worrying about my chances, I'd do something to improve them," Amir explains. "I'm going to start volunteering at an animal shelter. That way, when I finish school, I'll have some real-world experience. Maybe *you* could volunteer at, like, a soup kitchen or something. That'd be a way to help the homeless."

"Awesome idea!" Alyssa replies. "I think I'll talk to the volunteer coordinator at school. I bet she can tell me how I'd get started doing something like that."

The friends agree that volunteering is a great way to tackle both of their problems. Alyssa plans to make an appointment with the volunteer coordinator just as soon as she can. And Amir promises to make himself the best-prepared future vet he can be by totally committing himself to his volunteer work at the shelter.

Amir and Alyssa are like lots of teens across the United States— realizing that volunteering can help them feel good, solve problems, and meet their goals. Think volunteering might be a good fit for you? Read on to learn how volunteering can help you to help others, help yourself, learn about the world—and just have fun!

1 DOUBLE BONUS: HELP OTHERS— *and Yourself Too!*

Boosting people's moods and helping out the environment are both great things you can accomplish through volunteering.

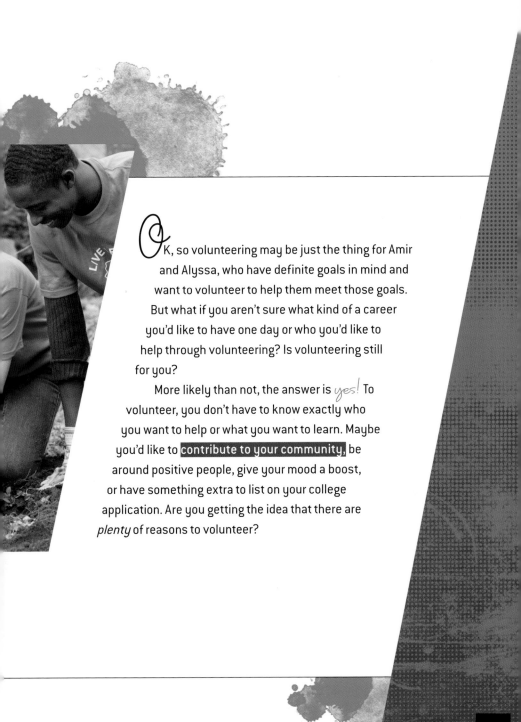

OK, so volunteering may be just the thing for Amir and Alyssa, who have definite goals in mind and want to volunteer to help them meet those goals. But what if you aren't sure what kind of a career you'd like to have one day or who you'd like to help through volunteering? Is volunteering still for you?

More likely than not, the answer is *yes!* To volunteer, you don't have to know exactly who you want to help or what you want to learn. Maybe you'd like to contribute to your community, be around positive people, give your mood a boost, or have something extra to list on your college application. Are you getting the idea that there are *plenty* of reasons to volunteer?

VOLUNTEERS

In 2010, 26 percent of all teens aged sixteen to nineteen volunteered, according to a survey by the Corporation for National and Community Service. But what did they do?

- About 34 percent volunteered at educational institutions, tutoring other students, assisting teachers and other staff, and pitching in with educational fund-raisers.
- About 31 percent helped out at a church, doing such things as assisting teachers of religion classes, caring for infants in a church nursery, or delivering food to homebound members of the church.
- About 14 percent volunteered in social services, collecting food for the needy, working in homeless shelters or soup kitchens, and mentoring younger kids.
- About 7 percent served in a hospital, helping staff or patients, stocking supplies, or directing visitors.
- About 4 percent volunteered in civic roles. They may have worked during public elections, helped to clean city parks or other public areas, or informed citizens about new laws or programs.
- About 3 percent helped with sports and arts. These volunteers might help a Little League coach with coaching duties, play catch with kids in need of mentors, or shadow a museum curator and assist with tasks at the museum.
- Another 7 percent found volunteer opportunities in other areas. They may have visited elderly people in nursing homes, helped at animal shelters, or raised funds for nonprofit organizations.

Of course, some teens volunteer because they have to. It may be a requirement for a class, a religious group, Boy Scouts or Girl Scouts, or even for high school graduation. But even teens who volunteer to meet a requirement usually get more than an academic credit or a scouting badge out of the experience. Indeed, many teens who have to volunteer find that once they get started volunteering, they don't want to stop.

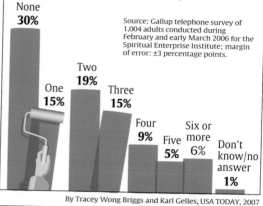

USA TODAY Snapshots®

Making A Difference

The 7 out of 10 adults who volunteer average 4.3 hours per week. Number of organizations adults volunteered with in the past year:

None
30%

Source: Gallup telephone survey of 1,004 adults conducted during February and early March 2006 for the Spiritual Enterprise Institute; margin of error: ±3 percentage points.

Two
19%

One
15%

Three
15%

Four
9%

Five
5%

Six or more
6%

Don't know/no answer
1%

By Tracey Wong Briggs and Karl Gelles, USA TODAY, 2007

For how many organizations does the average adult volunteer? This USA TODAY Snapshot® gives a pretty good idea.

Take a look at the following list of benefits that can come from volunteering. See which ones you're most interested in. Chances are that once you start volunteering, you'll find yourself rewarded in ways you didn't even imagine before you began!

IMPROVE THE WORLD: ONE PERSON, PET, OR PIECE OF LITTER AT A TIME

Changing the world may be the all-time number one reason for volunteering. Makes sense, right? Lots of people get into volunteering because they want to make a difference in the world. And whether

USA TODAY Snapshots®

What is a volunteer worth?

Nearly 62 million Americans do volunteer work:

Annual hours volunteered	**8 billion**
Value of volunteer time	**$162 billion**
Hourly value of volunteer time	**$20.25**

Source: Corporation for National and Community Service, based on Census data; Independent Sector

By Anne R. Carey and Sam Ward, USA TODAY, 2009

you're volunteering at an animal shelter, serving food to the hungry, or working to create stronger laws against littering, you're ultimately helping to make the world a better place.

Lots of teens get into volunteering so they can help people in their immediate community. They help younger kids with reading, math, and other homework. They help their peers by coaching or mentoring. They help low-income

Volunteers don't get paid, but that doesn't mean that their work doesn't have value. See the USA TODAY Snapshot® above to learn how valuable a volunteer's time really is.

Some teens help kids in their community with their homework.

families by collecting clothing and other household items. They help older people with yard work or visit lonely senior citizens at a retirement home. The list goes on and on. But the bottom line is that *lots of people can use your help in your community.*

But maybe helping *people* isn't really the thing that gets your blood flowing. Maybe you're more of an animal lover. You probably know there's a long list of animals in need. Unwanted pets need help. Abused animals *really* need help. And so do fish living in polluted waters. Again, the opportunities are endless.

Or maybe a greener Earth is your passion. Do you want to clean up the streets in your community or reduce garbage at a landfill? Get stricter pollution laws passed? Teen volunteers have been a huge part of the current environmental movement—and there's still plenty to do!

If you feel strongly about helping the environment, cleaning up the garbage in your community can be a great volunteering opportunity.

PRESIDENTIAL ENCOURAGEMENT

In April 2009, U.S. president Barack Obama called on all Americans to step up and serve their communities and their country. He signed the Edward M. Kennedy Serve America Act. This law—which builds on former laws passed in 1973 and 1990—expands national service programs and opportunities for Americans to volunteer. Obama said his goal is for all middle school, junior high, and high school students to complete fifty hours of community service per year.

President Barack Obama (left) signs the Edward M. Kennedy Serve America Act. On the right is Senator Edward Kennedy of Massachusetts.

FEEL GOOD

Who doesn't want to feel good about themselves? Let's face it—the good feelings you'll rack up from helping others are a huge reason to volunteer. Imagine how great you'll feel knowing that your actions are directly helping someone else stay warm, stay healthy, build confidence, beat loneliness, or any of the other thousands of results your volunteer activities can have on others. *It's a powerful feeling!* And once you experience it, you'll soon find that your own sense of self-esteem and confidence begins to grow. That's a win-win proposition!

Never underestimate the power of good feelings. They have the ability to improve—and even drastically change—your life. In fact, the times when you're feeling the most down may be the times when a self-esteem boost can help you the most. Are you going through a particularly rough time at home? Having problems with friends or teachers? This can be the best time to step away from your own problems a little bit and experience how good it feels to help others—or even just to stay busy! And as a bonus, helping others in need can help you put your problems into perspective. If you're dealing with homeless children, your lack of a new smartphone might not seem so tragic after all.

Helping others can make you feel good and improve your self-esteem.

USA TODAY

News

SECTION A

NEWS.USATODAY.COM

INTERNET SPURS
UPSWING IN VOLUNTEERISM

By Wendy Koch

Youth volunteerism is surging as high school and college students use the Internet to mobilize quickly and nationally. More than 22,000 non-profit groups have signed up to rally supporters on MySpace since it began in 2004, says Jeff Berman, the site's executive vice president for marketing. He says more young people are engaged in activism online and their creativity in using the Internet to do good works is "off the charts."

Groups also have sprung up on Facebook to urge youths to fight global warming, help Hurricane Katrina victims, seek world peace or protest events such as charges brought against six black teens in the beating of a white classmate in Jena, Louisiana.

"Activism is at a very high level among college students, probably more than in the last 10 to 20 years," says Robert Rhoads, who teaches a class on the history of student activism at the University of California, Los Angeles (UCLA). "There's a greater political consciousness among students," he says. "The Internet has played a role in that."

A growing number of college freshmen volunteer in their last year of high school, says John Pryor of the Higher Education Research Institute at UCLA. He found in a survey that 83 percent did so last year, up from 66 percent in 1989. Some high schools make community service a graduation requirement, but 70 percent of those who volunteered were not required to do so.

—March 13, 2008

IMPROVE YOUR FUTURE

Volunteering and taking action in your community doesn't have to be all about altruism (unselfishness). In fact, sometimes there's no better way to help yourself than by volunteering your time and talents.

A volunteer commitment can be the perfect opportunity to explore a career or learn a new skill. You can seek an opportunity in a specific field you're interested in exploring. For instance, an art student might volunteer at a museum. Or someone planning to be a doctor or a nurse might volunteer at a hospital. But remember that you'll gain valuable skills in just about any volunteer experience. Whether it's working with people, solving problems on your own, or mastering new computer software, the work you do as a volunteer will pay you back throughout your career.

And when it's time to apply to college or for a job, you'll find that having some real-world experience can really help your chances. Admissions officers and employers are often impressed

If you want to work in the medical field in the future, volunteering at a hospital can help you get experience in that field.

by the extras you have on your application. Colleges are increasingly looking beyond grades and test scores to figure out who would be the best fit for their schools. And employers almost always value any work experience—paid or unpaid. Volunteer experience can communicate two things to both colleges and employers. It can show that you're a hard worker who likes to take on challenges and try new things. And it can show experience in specific fields. So make sure you highlight your volunteer experience on your résumés and college applications.

NEW IDEAS,
NEW SKILLS, NEW FRIENDS

Even if you're not specifically looking to brush up your college applications, volunteering can help you figure out your interests, your skills, and even your life's direction. Is there something you've always wanted to explore? There's probably a volunteer experience that can help you learn about it. Have no idea what you want to do with your life? Try volunteering in a few different settings to learn a little about what you like—and don't like—to do.

Sometimes you don't even know what you want to explore. You just realize that maybe you're ready to try something new. Do you ever find yourself sitting around bored to death? Then you're a prime candidate to volunteer!

Volunteering can help you beat boredom by giving you something fun and rewarding to do.

Want to spend more time with the elderly? Some teens coordinate with churches or other organizations to help out senior citizens in their own homes. Retirement communities also often seek out volunteers.

One more thing: volunteering can also help you meet lots of different people. This can be great if you've just moved to an area or are feeling as if you could stand to mix up your social circle. Plus, the people you'll meet while volunteering will probably have different things to offer than do most of your peers in school. For instance, if you don't have any grandparents or other senior citizens in your life, residents of a retirement community can help fill that void. Or if you've always wanted to see what it would be like to work as a park ranger, volunteering alongside one can be a great opportunity to learn the ropes from a pro. Lots of volunteers say that one of their biggest rewards is getting to know people from different walks of life. Whatever your choice of volunteer work, you're almost sure to meet someone you wouldn't have otherwise met.

2 GET OUT THERE: HOW TO FIND a Volunteer Opportunity

One way to find a volunteer opportunity is to contact a group such as the Red Cross.

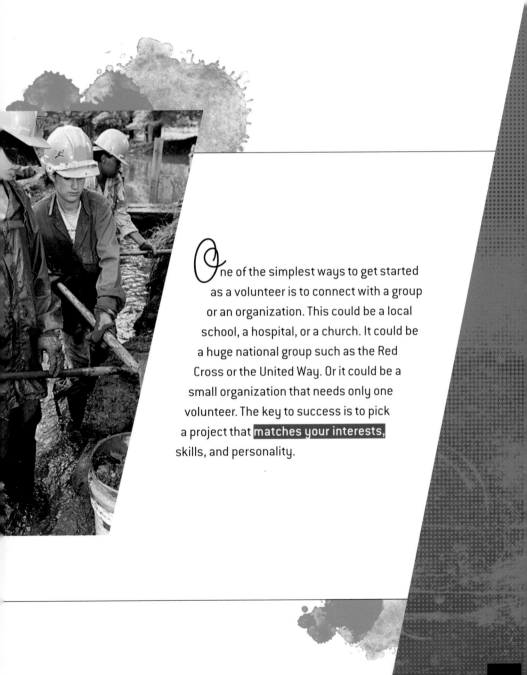

One of the simplest ways to get started as a volunteer is to connect with a group or an organization. This could be a local school, a hospital, or a church. It could be a huge national group such as the Red Cross or the United Way. Or it could be a small organization that needs only one volunteer. The key to success is to pick a project that matches your interests, skills, and personality.

GET STARTED

It's not hard to find a volunteer opportunity. There's one *waiting for the right volunteer* in just about every field you can imagine. Some are advertised on TV, on billboards, or on the Internet. But many others are never advertised. You've got to go out and find them yourself. One great way to get started is at a website that lets you search through opportunities at many different organizations. Try one of the sites at on the next page, or type "find a volunteer opportunity" into a search engine.

Some organizations specialize in matching volunteers with opportunities. Your school or place of worship may have a volunteer coordinator. Or you can try a national group such as the Boys & Girls Clubs of America (www.bgca.org) that helps match teens to volunteer opportunities. If you're seventeen or older, check AmeriCorps (www.americorps.gov) to find out about community service projects where you can also earn money for college.

One way to find volunteering opportunities is to check your local newspaper.

SEARCH FOR VOLUNTEER OPPORTUNITIES

Idealist

http://www.idealist.org

This nonprofit group offers a searchable "idea list" of volunteer opportunities around the world.

Volunteer Match

http://www.volunteermatch.org

This nonprofit, online service helps you search for local opportunities that match your skills and interests. This site even has a section for opportunities that are great for teens.

Youth Volunteer Corps of America

http://www.yvca.org

This nonprofit group has offices in dozens of cities throughout the United States. Visit www.yvca.org/locate .php to see if there's one near you. If there is, you can contact the office directly.

HOW DO YOU WANT TO MAKE A DIFFERENCE?

Have an idea of how or where you'd like to make a difference? Check out these lists of ideas by interest or skill areas.

Affecting Public Policy
- Hand out pamphlets for a political candidate or policy group.
- Join a group with a cause you support.

Helping Animals
- Clean kennels or walk dogs at an animal shelter.
- Write articles or take photographs for an animal shelter's newsletter or website.

Helping Low-Income People
- Collect food for a food shelf.
- Help at a homeless shelter or a soup kitchen.

Helping People with Health Challenges
- Visit hospice patients.
- Spend time with kids at a children's hospital.

Helping with Natural Disasters
- Help sandbag an area when flooding is expected.
- Join a Red Cross relief effort.

Improving the Environment
- Help at a recycling center.
- Volunteer at a state park.

This teen prepares to hand a sandbag to another volunteer. He's working to prepare a town for an expected flood.

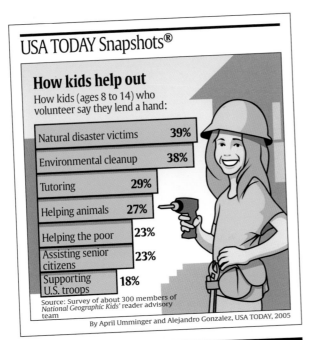

USA TODAY Snapshots®

How kids help out
How kids (ages 8 to 14) who volunteer say they lend a hand:

Natural disaster victims	39%
Environmental cleanup	38%
Tutoring	29%
Helping animals	27%
Helping the poor	23%
Assisting senior citizens	23%
Supporting U.S. troops	18%

Source: Survey of about 300 members of *National Geographic Kids'* reader advisory team

By April Umminger and Alejandro Gonzalez, USA TODAY, 2005

Websites and service organizations are great ways to discover volunteering options you may never have even thought of. But what if you already know exactly where you want to volunteer? Then it might be best to go straight to the source. Call the organization—

So how exactly do kids volunteer? Check out the USA TODAY Snapshot® above for a quick breakdown of the types of volunteering opportunities in which young people take part.

or visit in person—and say that you want to help. Odds are, they'll be happy to put you to work!

MAKE SURE IT'S RIGHT FOR YOU

It's easy to get excited about the thought of making a difference. But be careful. Don't be tempted to jump too quickly into the first volunteer opportunity you find. Make sure it's right for you. Does the work fit your personality? Do you have the time you need to devote to the organization? Will it interest you enough that you'll stick with it?

Try to find at least two to three options for your volunteer work. Get as much information about each option as you can. You'll want

If you find an organization for which you'd like to volunteer, set up a meeting with the person in charge to learn more.

to know the time commitment, schedules, responsibilities, tasks, and who you'll be working with. Try to set up at least a brief talk with the person who will be in charge. Be wary if a group says you don't need to interview. They should be as interested in making sure you are a good fit for the opportunity as you are.

Once you've gathered information, make a decision. Discuss your thoughts with a teacher, a counselor, a relative, or another adult. Above all, make sure you don't overcommit yourself. Remember your school, family, and work obligations. If an opportunity fits into your schedule and it feels right for you, give it a try.

WHAT SKILLS CAN YOU USE TO MAKE A DIFFERENCE?

Have an idea of how or where you'd like to make a difference? Check out these lists of ideas by interest or skill areas.

I'm a good listener
- Help staff a crises-call help line.
- Visit a senior center.

I'm artistic
- Plan art projects with an after-school program.
- Teach an art class at a homeless shelter.

I'm good at fixing things
- Repair small appliances at a nonprofit thrift store.
- Help an organization keep its equipment running smoothly.

I'm good with computers
- Build or maintain a website for a small nonprofit group.
- Help an organization with tech support.

I'm good with younger kids
- Volunteer at a crisis nursery.
- Tutor kids after school.

I'm skilled at building things
- Build houses with Habitat for Humanity.
- Help build playground equipment for a homeless shelter or an after-school group.

I have a flair for fashion
- Plan window displays at a nonprofit thrift store.
- Help women plan outfits with a group that donates work-appropriate clothing (such as pantsuits, skirts, and blouses) to low-income working women.

I like to garden
- Plant and maintain flower beds at a homeless shelter.
- Do yard work or gardening for elderly neighbors.

TEENS REACH OUT
TO HELP OTHERS AT HOME, GLOBALLY

By Sharon Jayson

Despite what you may have heard, tweens aren't all about social networking, iPods, the mall, and celebrities. Growing numbers of preteens and early teens are giving tweens a new face: a socially responsible young citizen. They're not only doing good in their local communities, but they're also having a global impact. Some have created their own non-profits, and most have websites enlisting the support of kids like themselves who also want to help others.

KATIE'S KROPS

Katie was just 9 and in third grade when her gardening skills for a school project enabled her to produce a 40-pound [18-kilogram] cabbage that fed 275 people and launched her efforts to feed the hungry. "Helping all those people who have to come to soup kitchens and homeless shelters is [the main] reason I like this project," says Katie, 12, a sixth-grader from Summerville, S.C. Her website, katieskrops.com, helps kids fight hunger.

[Katie's mother], Stacy, 41, says her daughter oversees six gardens, including a large garden at her school. "I'm always a believer that if a child shows an interest in something, you nurture it and support it," Stacy says.

LEMONAID WARRIORS

Lulu's idea for lemonade stands to raise money grew out of the [2010] earthquake in Haiti. At her school, she suggested that the girls and boys compete in a "lemonade war" to raise money. Now her organization is becoming a non-profit. It just launched lemonaidwarriors.com.

"It gives me this very good feeling inside that I just put a big smile on someone's face," says Lulu, 11, a sixth-grader from California. Her mother, Lisa, 46, advises parents to "empower your kids and help them work for charities that mean something to them."

(LULU CERONE)

A sixth grader named Lulu started a non-profit called LemonAID Warriors. You can learn more online at www.lemonaidwarriors.com.

"They naturally want to give and naturally want to help," she says. "Teach them to respect that desire. Teach them the value of a small idea. It'll grow from there."

GOODY GOODIES

Macallan, 15, is a high school sophomore in Poughkeepsie, New York. She was just 11 when her family returned from three years in Botswana, and she couldn't forget the hungry orphans who rummaged through garbage for food. She started raising money to help the children, which turned into the sale of fair-trade products [products purchased from small producers at fair prices] both online at her non-profit site, GoodyGoodies.org, and at her mother's fair-trade store. "Mom always helps people. She's great about that," Macallan says.

Her mother, Cecilia, 47, says it's "a parent's job to expose [their children] to ways they can positive[ly] impact the world. . . . It's just a matter of listening and fostering the things that are of interest to your child. It's our job to create avenues for our children to succeed."

—*October 14, 2010*

You don't get paid for a volunteer experience, but in just about every other way, it's a job. Do yourself—and your fellow volunteers—a favor and treat it as one. This means you should follow basic workplace rules. These include the following:

- Show up on time.
- Dress appropriately.
- Use appropriate language and discretion.
- Ask questions upfront.
- Don't complain to colleagues.
- Find out the accepted method for reporting complaints or making suggestions.

First Lady Michelle Obama *(center)* helps paint a house for the needy with other volunteers. Volunteering can be very rewarding.

That may sound like a lot of rules, but they're pretty simple. Remember, the main thing is to *enjoy your experience and act respectfully toward others.* That way you'll gain more from your volunteering experience—and those you volunteer with and for will gain more from you as well. Soon you'll be on the road to a lifetime of rewarding volunteer activities.

3 TAKE CHARGE!: START YOUR OWN
Service Project

If you're a take-charge type of person, you might consider starting your own service project.

Are you more of a take-charge character than a go-with-the-flow personality? Do you enjoy taking on leadership positions? If this sounds like you, then you might be a good candidate for starting your own volunteering venture.

Starting a volunteering project can be *a hugely rewarding experience.* Of course, it can also be enormously complicated! It can be easy to bite off more than you can chew.

WHAT'S SERVICE LEARNING?

You may have a formal service learning program at your school—or maybe you've heard the term at your church or in an after-school group. But what exactly *is* service learning? Actually, service learning is a lot of things. It means any program or project that combines learning with hands-on community service work. The goal is for students to apply what they learn in the classroom to a real-life experience—and to make their community a little better.

Service learning projects can include a whole school, one or more classrooms, or even one student. Usually some part of classroom learning, reading, and writing are required as well as a certain amount of hands-on volunteer work that students perform. For instance, students in a civics class might research the issue of homelessness in their community. Then they might complete a paper describing a proposed solution. Finally, they may volunteer a certain number of hours at a homeless shelter. Does your school have any service learning projects, or can you think of some you'd like to see put in action?

But this doesn't mean that you should be afraid to start a project. It just means you should take it slow—at least at first. Break it down into manageable steps, and ask for help when you need it. Take a look at the sample steps here to get an idea of how you can tackle your own project.

STEP 1: DO YOUR RESEARCH

If you already know that you want to start your own service project, then you might also have a pretty good idea of what you want to do—or at least which issue or problem you want to tackle. But if you don't, then this step can help you to identify your goal. Get started by asking some key questions:

- What are the biggest issues facing your community—or the world?
- What are your own interests? What gets you excited?
- What are your skills? What are you good at?
- What's the best way to address an issue or problem you're concerned about?

You might notice that there are two kinds of questions here—those that make you think about the problem you want to address and those that make you think about yourself. That's because a successful project needs to be **focused on a key issue,** but it also needs to be a good fit for you and your particular skills and interests. You'll reap the rewards later if you take the time to think about both of these issues upfront.

STEP 2: SET A GOAL

Once you've got your basic idea for a project, think about the specifics. Ask yourself some more questions:

- How much time can I spend on this project?
- How many other people should I involve?
- How much money or other resources am I willing or able to commit to the project?

The answers to these questions will help you decide how big a problem you're equipped to tackle. They may also help you identify an even more specific goal to aim for in your project. For example, imagine that your goal is to clean up graffiti around your neighborhood. Should you aim to clean up everything in your town or city? Or should you focus mostly on your block or your surrounding neighborhood? Knowing exactly how much time, assistance, and money you have will help you set a realistic goal. Remember that you can always expand your goals later on. *Start with something you can handle!*

If your goal is to clean up graffiti, figure out how much of the city you aim to clean. You can always start small and expand later.

HOW DO YOU WANT TO MAKE A DIFFERENCE?

Helping Animals
- Start a network to help find homes for pets in an animal shelter.
- Organize a group of friends to volunteer at a local zoo or animal shelter.

Helping Low-Income People
- Hold a food drive or start a community garden and donate to a shelter or food shelf.
- Assemble and donate care packages to a homeless shelter.

Helping People with Health Issues
- Start a buddy-matching program at your school. Match students with senior citizens, chronically ill kids, or others who need companions.
- Start an after-school fitness program.

Helping with Natural Disasters
- Organize an outing to clean up storm damage.
- Assemble and distribute care packages for people displaced by a disaster.

Improving the Environment
- Set up a neighborhood action group to help clean vacant lots, pick up litter, or remove graffiti.
- Organize a school cleanup day.

For most service projects, it's helpful to involve a team of peers and at least one adult.

STEP 3: FORM A TEAM

OK, you've got your idea and you've set some goals. It's time to form your team! Your team may be just you. But for most projects, it's helpful to have at least another person or two.

You might also want to bring at least one adult in on your team. Even if the adult doesn't actively take part, he or she can serve as an adviser or a sponsor. An adviser helps you come up with ideas and offers opinions on how to improve what you're doing. A sponsor, meanwhile, allows you to use his or her name to gain credibility when speaking to other adults. It's not really fair, but some adults will take you seriously only if they know your project has some adult supervision.

STEP 4:
WHO ARE YOU HELPING?

It's easy to get carried away with your excitement over your service project. But don't ever forget the reason you're doing it—to help people. Those who will benefit from your service are called recipients. If you're setting out to clothe the homeless, then homeless people are your recipients. If you want to start a tutoring service, the kids being tutored are the recipients. Of course, if your goal is to clean up garbage in your town, there are no direct recipients. Then you can skip this step.

So what do your recipients want or need out of your service? Don't just guess. *Ask them!* You can do this by talking to people, conducting a survey, or even reading up on an issue. Check out these examples:

- If you want to collect shoes for a homeless shelter, you can call or e-mail the shelter's director to ask about their specific needs.
- If you want to help feed people in a neighborhood made up mostly of Somali families, you can research Somalian foods and conduct a survey or a few interviews to find out what food staples your recipients need most.
- If you're offering a product or a service to people, you can find out when and where they are available to receive it. For example, say you're planning to tutor kids from several different schools. Do they need tutors at school, at home, or somewhere else?

STEP 5: GET ORGANIZED

Now, it's time to get down to details! Before you start working, you need to figure out the who, what, when, where, and how of the plan. Think about these details:

- **Setting dates.** How long will your project last? If you can, try to set a specific start and end date. You can always extend it for another "round" once you reach your end date.
- **Team roles.** If you recruited partners, helpers, or advisers, you'll want to make sure you identify everyone's role. If you can, have a planning meeting where you all agree on who will be responsible for what and how much time you each expect to commit.
- **A day-to-day schedule.** Yeah, yeah, schedules are a pain, but you're going to need one. Figure out when things need to be done and when people are expected to take part, and write it all down so everyone's on the same page.

STEP 6: RAISE FUNDS

If your project is going to need more than you can personally donate in supplies or cash, *you may need to raise funds.* There are all kinds of ways to do this. You can hold a bake sale or a garage sale, you can ask people directly for donations, or you can even try writing a grant proposal. What's that? A grant proposal is a formal request for money to fund a specific project. You'll have to find out who gives out grants for your type of project (a government agency or a nonprofit group is the most likely candidate), then send a detailed description of your project and an explaination how the money would be used. Does writing a grant proposal sound a little terrifying? Well, never fear! You can find lots of good tips for writing one by simply entering "how to write a grant proposal" in a search engine.

Even if you don't need cold cash, you might need to raise support from your community. For instance, you might want to ask a business or a group to donate a meeting space or provide coffee to your recipients or help in some other way. Usually individuals and businesses love to help out on service projects—especially if you come to them with a well-thought-out plan and a request that's not too crazy.

STEP 7: REACH OUT

What good is a service project if nobody knows about it? *It's time to do a little marketing!* You don't need a big-budget advertising campaign to do this. Just reach out to people. Talk to business owners, government officials, neighbors, or even just people on the street. You could consider printing some fliers to pin up on public bulletin boards; sending a press release to your local newspaper, TV station, or radio station; or even announcing your plans on Facebook, Twitter, or another social networking website.

One way to advertise your service project is to post fliers on public bulletin boards.

Maybe you've heard of red tape—all those little formal details you have to slog through before you can finish something. Red tape sometimes includes doing paperwork, such as filling out forms, or getting formal permission from the government to hold an event or stage a fund-raiser. *Yuck!* It's an easy part of the process to put off or overlook, but don't fall into that trap. Since the last thing you want is to have your project shut down once you start rolling, you'll want to do a little digging to see if there's any red tape you need to cut through.

You might be scratching your head, wondering what exactly we're talking about here. Consider this example. You're planning to help a local animal shelter by raising money with a car wash. You need to make sure you have permission to use a public area for your car wash. You may need to find out if you need a permit to collect money for a nonprofit agency. And you'll certainly need to check with the shelter first to make sure they actually want you to do the fund-raiser! Welcome to red tape.

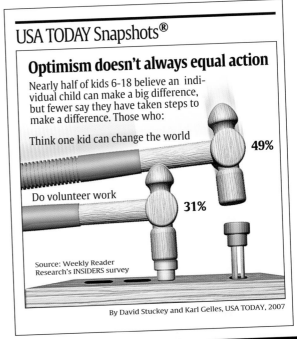

USA TODAY Snapshots®

Optimism doesn't always equal action

Nearly half of kids 6-18 believe an individual child can make a big difference, but fewer say they have taken steps to make a difference. Those who:

Think one kid can change the world — 49%

Do volunteer work — 31%

Source: Weekly Reader Research's INSIDERS survey

By David Stuckey and Karl Gelles, USA TODAY, 2007

Almost half of kids believe that they can make a difference, but as the above USA TODAY Snapshot® shows, less than a third of them actually volunteer.

STEP 9: ENJOY!

Starting a service project requires lots of work, organization, and commitment. But remember the reason you started your project—to make a difference and have some fun helping others! Take the time to enjoy the reward of feeling great by helping to change the world. And take note of your successes. Keep a log of your achievements. This will be a great way to remind yourself of all you've accomplished. It can also be useful if you plan to start another service project down the road. Most of all, be proud of yourself—*you're making a difference!*

STEP 10: REFLECT

It's always a good idea to think about how well you're doing and what you can learn for the future. If you're working with a group, you can plan a group reflection meeting. Everyone can have a chance to comment on what they think is working well, what their challenges are, and what they'd like to see in the future. Then you can use those comments to brainstorm ideas for improving your project in the future.

Starting a service project is a lot of work. Don't forget to have fun while helping others.

TEENS STEP UP
TO GIVE HOMELESS KIDS SHOES

By Nanci Hellmich

When he was 5 years old, Nick of Cranston, Rhode Island, started going to homeless shelters with his mother, Lori, who works at shelters as an art therapist. On his first visit, he noticed that many kids didn't have decent clothing or shoes. When he got home, he went through his own closet, grabbed gently used clothes and shoes that no longer fit him, as well as toys and games, and he and his mother took the items back to the shelter.

He gave one child a pair of winter boots, but they were too big, and Nick felt bad. He also noticed that some kids shared their shoes with other family members.

So in 2010, at age 12, Nick decided to collect new shoes for homeless children as a community service project. He and his parents, Daniel and Lori, created the non-profit Gotta Have Sole Foundation (gottahavesole.org). The foundation has given shoes to 800 homeless children in shelters in Rhode Island and Washington, D.C. The footwear is donated by shoe manufacturers, retailers, churches, synagogues, and individuals.

Running the foundation is a family affair with the volunteer help of his mother, father and grandparents. Nick has delivered all the shoes in person, often lacing them up for little ones. "Some children can't put their shoes on their feet by themselves. They ask me to do that, and I'm more than happy to."

Homeless shelter personnel send requests for sizes and types of shoes, and Nick's family tries to find the right pairs in the stockpile they have in their garage. "If we don't have it, we go get it," Nick says. "We don't turn anybody down, because they deserve shoes as much as anybody else."

The reactions are heartwarming. One time a young mother with two sons "came over and hugged me and squeezed me tight, and she was crying. She thanked me so much for thinking of her family and helping her," Nick says.

His mother says this entire endeavor, the foundation's name, and even the logo were her son's ideas. "His passion has fueled us to pave the way for him

Check out Gotta Have Sole's web page at www.gottahavesole.org to find out all about how the organization helps the homeless.

to continue," she says. On the other hand, she tries to make sure her son has a balanced life. "It's essential that he is a normal 13-year-old pursuing his other interests."

Nick works for the Gotta Have Sole Foundation about 10 hours a week, which leaves him plenty of time to study, play tennis, and play the bass guitar in a band and jazz ensemble. To those considering doing volunteer work, Nick says: "It doesn't matter what you do or how long you do it."

—*July 13, 2011*

4 SAY IT LOUD: HOW TO MAKE Your Voice Heard

Protesters are activists. Being an activist is one way to make your voice heard.

$\mathcal{T}$here's no doubt about it—doing volunteer or service project work is a powerful way to make a difference in the world. But it's not the only way. If there's an issue you're passionate about, you can work to make people think more about it and even try to convince lawmakers to pass laws that support your idea. That's right—*you can be an activist.*

Maybe you've seen activists in your community or on television. Antiwar protesters are activists. So is the woman asking for your signature on a petition at the grocery store. And so is the high-strung guy shouting into a megaphone on a busy street. An activist is simply someone who acts on their values and beliefs and then works to convince others to share and act on those same beliefs. They use their words and actions to stick up for the causes they believe in.

HOW DO YOU WANT TO MAKE A DIFFERENCE?

Helping Animals

- Create a flier encouraging people to spay or neuter their pets to reduce the population of stray animals.
- Learn about animal research practices, and discuss your findings with a school or a neighborhood group.

Helping Low-Income People

- Lobby your state and local representatives for better job-training programs, low-income housing programs, or other projects.
- Start a petition in your school to encourage your state legislators to support health care and other services for low-income families.

Helping People with Health Challenges

- Spread awareness about the importance of regular dental and doctor checkups.
- Start a campaign against drug and alcohol abuse.

Helping with Natural Disasters

- Raise awareness of victims' needs after a disaster.
- Lobby your representative for benefits and assistance to aid disaster victims.

Improving the Environment

- Write a letter to the editor about an environmental hazard in your community.
- Encourage your representatives to support bills that help the

Sounds great, right? But can one teen really make a difference? Maybe it sometimes seems as if adults don't really listen to teens. And it's true—sometimes it's easy for people in power to assume that teens don't know what they're talking about. But *you do have power as a teen.* Read on to learn about ways that you can become an activist for the causes that matter to you.

DO YOUR RESEARCH

The first step to being an activist is to do your research. Learn the truth about the issues that interest you. This sounds simple, but beware of false information. Remember that usually people on both sides of a debate feel passionately about their positions. And so sometimes they distort facts, exaggerate, or even spread outright lies to support their position. It's up to you to separate the truth from the lies—and that's not always easy.

So what can you do? Arm yourself with the facts behind any issue. The Internet is a great place to start, but be wary of getting caught up in information overload or of getting caught up reading sites that present only biased views on the issue. An Internet search for "animal testing," "gay and lesbian rights," or "air pollution" will turn up seemingly endless information and not all of it good. To keep on track, try reading a few summaries by people on both sides of the issue. Don't just focus on sites that support your position. The best way to argue against an opposing position is to understand it. If you're willing to learn only about one side, you're not really going to be very informed, are you? Take notes, research questionable or unusual facts, and try to get to the truth. Again, search engines are your friend. Type a few keywords into a search engine and see what you find. Or hit the local library to ask about database subscriptions that you can access. If possible, use government sites to verify your facts.

Talking about your issue is a great way to spread the word.

Once you've boned up on the issue, chances are you'll be ready to take action. Maybe you found one specific piece of the issue that really angers you, frustrates you, or motivates you. That's the piece you'll want to focus on as you begin your activism. You can choose from tons of ways to act on your beliefs. Below are a few common ways to work for change.

SPREAD THE WORD

It's time to spread the word about whatever issue you've chosen. This is what activism is really all about. But how are you supposed to do it? You've got numerous choices. Here are just a few:

- **Talk!** Your voice is your most powerful tool. Once you're sure of the facts, discuss your issue with anybody who's interested—friends, family, neighbors . . . anyone who's willing to listen.

USA TODAY Snapshots®

A digital generation gap

Adults who say the impact of blogs and chat rooms on uniting people to make a difference in the world is slight or nonexistent:

Age group

- 18-39 — **29%**
- 40-54 — **35%**
- 55 and older — **50%**

Source: American Express survey of 1,000 adults conducted online by ICR and Authentic Response

By Anne R. Carey and Keith Simmons, USA TODAY, 2008

More and more people are getting inspired to make a difference through blogs and other online resources. But as this USA TODAY Snapshot® shows, not everyone views these online resources in the same light. Young people tend to put more stock in them than older people.

Note the key word *interested*. As an activist, you'll have to learn the appropriate time and tone for talking about your issues. Most people don't want to hear a lecture. And they don't want to be criticized endlessly either. It's fine to state your opinion— once or twice— about the fact that your parents drive a gas-guzzling SUV or that your friend wastes plastic products at lunch, but unless you have something new to share, there's no need to keep bringing it up. If your issue is something that you feel a certain group could really benefit from, you might want to hold a group meeting, for example, with younger kids, to talk about bullying.

- **Post fliers.** This may be the simplest way to spread a message. You can simply write down what you want people to know: "Keep our rivers and lakes clean: don't litter." Or "Thousands of dogs and cats are homeless and hungry. Prevent overpopulation by spaying or neutering your pet today." You can put your fliers on public bulletin boards at places such as community centers, coffeehouses, and the library.

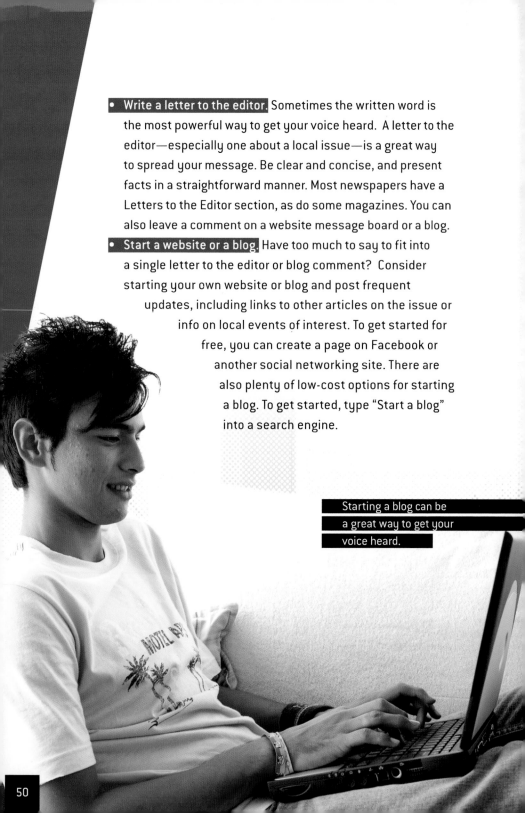

- **Write a letter to the editor.** Sometimes the written word is the most powerful way to get your voice heard. A letter to the editor—especially one about a local issue—is a great way to spread your message. Be clear and concise, and present facts in a straightforward manner. Most newspapers have a Letters to the Editor section, as do some magazines. You can also leave a comment on a website message board or a blog.
- **Start a website or a blog.** Have too much to say to fit into a single letter to the editor or blog comment? Consider starting your own website or blog and post frequent updates, including links to other articles on the issue or info on local events of interest. To get started for free, you can create a page on Facebook or another social networking site. There are also plenty of low-cost options for starting a blog. To get started, type "Start a blog" into a search engine.

Starting a blog can be a great way to get your voice heard.

SHOP YOUR CONSCIENCE

Want to send a message to big companies? The magic word here is *money*! You control where you spend it, and that's a powerful way to send a message. Shopping your conscience means spending your money on things you value, and—even more important—not spending it on things that you feel are bad for the environment, the community, or other people or animals. To really make an impact, *you can start or join a boycott*. In this form of activism, people join together to refuse to buy a product or a group of products as a way to protest a company or an industry. You might boycott fur coats, meat products, gas-guzzling cars, nonrecyclable plastics(below), or cosmetics tested

Ingredients: Sunflower oil, castor oil, beeswax, candelilla w
lanolin, cocoa seed butter, tocopheryl acetate & tocopher
(vitamin E), peppermint oil, carnauba wax, rosemary leaf
May contain: iron oxide, mica, carmine or titanium dioxic

Not tested on animals 100% NATL

.0975 oz. (2.6 g)
Customer Inquiry Hotline

This lip care product is marked "Not tested on animals." Some people choose not to spend money on products that are tested on animals.

on animals. By refusing to spend your money on products you don't believe in, you're letting companies know that you don't approve of their practices.

Think people don't really care what teens spend their money on? Think again! Teens spend more than $100 billion a year. Put it all together and that's a powerful voice. You may not have a lot of money. But think about what you spend it on. For most teens, it's discretionary items—or items that you don't have to buy but choose to. Think designer clothes, video games, music, snacks, and so on. Companies know you have choices. *Let them know what matters to you.*

So how exactly can you send a message with your wallet? In tons of ways. Worried about plastics building up in landfills? Take action by refusing to buy individual bottles of water. Fed up with degrading messages from popular singers or bands? Don't buy their music or concert tickets. Worried about the treatment of chickens on huge poultry farms? Talk to your parents about buying free-range poultry (poultry not confined to cages or buildings) or cage-free eggs. Free-range poultry and cage-free eggs are sometimes a little more expensive than food products from huge farms. But you could even offer to donate some of the extra cost to the family grocery budget. There are probably lots of ways that you can make a difference just by making small changes to your shopping habits.

LOBBY YOUR LEGISLATORS

Ready to kick your activism into high gear? You—yes, even you, a lowly, nonvoting teenager!—can get your voice heard by your government representatives by lobbying them about your issue. This means you try to convince them to support your cause. If there's already a bill—a proposal for a new law—about your issue, then you might try to convince them to vote yes or no on the bill. But if there's no active bill, you can still lobby your representative so that he or she knows how you feel in case a bill does come up for a vote.

You can lobby at the local (city, town, or county) level, at the state or province level, or to the federal government. State and provincial governments often deal with issues involving the environment, health, education, and other areas of interest to teens. In the United States, every state has a legislature that makes state laws. In many states, these legislatures are part-time bodies. They meet only some months of the year or even every other year. Check with your state to see when your legislature is in session—that is, when they are actively debating and voting on bills. Even if your legislature is not formally in session, you can usually still lobby your representative, but it helps to know the annual schedule.

These students meet with government representatives about an issue regarding tuition.

A MOMENT OF "TRUTH"
SET ONE TEEN ON A PATH OF ACTIVISM

By Gail Sheehy

So, what have you done lately about global warming? Not much, right? Why?

Because you're a busy grown-up. I'm pitching my hopes with youth. I'm betting on a 16-year-old revolutionary who was fired up by Al Gore and inspired by the words of Thomas Jefferson: "Every generation needs a new revolution."

Alec was 12 when his mother nudged him to see a boring documentary that changed his life. Up until then, Alec had been a regular kid, goofing off in class, his primary concern being how much he could level up in his favorite video game.

"Seeing [the global-warming documentary] *An Inconvenient Truth* changed my life forever," the tall, lanky teenager tells audiences. He applied to Gore's organization to train as a presenter of Gore's slide show. *Rejected. Too young.* So Alec created his own slide show and traveled around California with it. When he was finally able to meet the former vice president, Gore was happy to send him off as the youngest of his trained ambassadors.

Who says only experienced adults can have a vision? Alec thinks globally. He started a non-profit organization, Kids Versus Global Warming, and has spent his early teen years organizing the iMatter March for the week of Mother's Day. From May 7-14, his kid activists plan to send shock waves around the world as they take to the streets of their communities.

Middle school and high school students will be the march organizers, working with their parents, grandparents, teachers, coaches, and local leaders to make that week one when people of all ages from across the globe stand up to protect the world and preserve the climate for young and future generations.

"I've realized in my work that our problem with fossil fuels is bigger than just climate change," Alec says. "Really, it's about living as if the future matters."

As socially awkward as any gawky 16-year-old boy, Alec has developed himself into an electrifying speaker. His passion fires up not only his peers, but also their parents and supporters, such as Robert Redford and Ted Turner, the Sierra Club and the U.S. Green Building Council.

Al Gore promotes his movie *An Inconvenient Truth*. Alec from California was inspired by the film and applied to train as a presenter of Gore's slide show.

"There's a lot of ageism against young people," Alec says. "Even at climate change conferences with cool people who care, they assume that young people don't matter. But we do matter.

"I'm just a regular kid who isn't rich or brilliant, but I found my passion and I went with it. Young people are some of the most creative and dedicated activists now. We have no official political power, we can't even vote. But we have a voice. It's not about money or power—it's about the future of our generation and survival of the planet."

Alec has an uncommonly civil relationship with his mother, Victoria Loorz, who usually but not always travels with him and arranges for his home-schooling.

Alec stresses that a young leader need not be experienced; this event will train him or her for activism that can be built on for the rest of life.

—*April 19, 2009*

To get started, you'll want to build a team of supporters. Shoot for a good variety—a mix of young and old is great. If you can get ethnic or racial diversity, even better. You might even convince a lawmaker to support your cause. This gives you instant credibility! Research the backgrounds of your representatives to find a likely candidate. Write letters to introduce yourself, and clearly explain what kind of help you're seeking. It may seem like a long shot, but you never know—you might just make a powerful ally!

Knowing when your issue is up for discussion is important. Lobbying is really only effective when an issue is coming up for a vote. Most state legislatures have websites with posted schedules of committee agendas, or the topics and bills up for discussion that day.

Contact a representative before a senate committee meeting and ask to speak. Speaking at a committee meeting is a great way to have your voice heard.

Make sure you stay on top of your issue by closely following this committee calendar.

One powerful way to make your voice heard is to show up for committee meetings. The rules on this vary from state to state, so check your own state legislature for its policies. If you do visit a legislative committee, you can sometimes bring a poster briefly stating your opinion on the issue. Sometimes you can carry these into committee meetings or hold them in the hallways outside of meetings. You can also print copies of a one-page summary of your position on the issue. You can hand these out to representatives and other interested parties before the meetings. You can also contact your representative beforehand to ask whether you can speak during the meeting.

If you can't make it to your state legislature, you can still lobby by phone, e-mail, or mail. Send brief, clear statements of your support to key lawmakers. You'll find their contact information on the legislature's website. You can also start a petition, get it filled up with signatures, and send it to the lawmakers who will vote on the bill.

EPILOGUE
BE TOMORROW'S *Leader*

This teen volunteers with an organization that paints murals on empty buildings in the city. By volunteering, you are not only helping your community but yourself as well.

Being a volunteer or an activist can be simple. Spend twenty minutes with a senior citizen, clean out a few dog kennels at a rescue shelter, spend an afternoon picking up trash at a local park, or sign a petition for cleaner air or better schools. All of those actions work to improve your community. The point is not how much you do— it's that you make an effort.

Every time you donate your time to a cause you believe in, you're working for change. You're benefiting others as well as yourself—most volunteers agree that they grow from the experience in ways they never imagined. By showing your passion and support for a cause, you're showing adults everywhere that teens really do care about improving the world around them.

Teenage volunteers and activists are showing with their actions today that they're prepared to be the leaders of tomorrow. And that gets noticed by their peers, their families, the colleges they want to go to, and the employers they hope will one day hire them.

When you take the first step to volunteering with a group, starting a service project, or becoming an activist, you join that group of tomorrow's leaders. You're preparing to make yourself and the world you live in a better place.

GLOSSARY

ACTIVIST: a person who acts on his or her beliefs and encourages others to do the same

ALTRUISM: acting for the good of others rather than one's self

BLOG: a frequently updated website where a person or people share their thoughts and beliefs on issues or events. *Blog* is short for Weblog.

DISCRETIONARY: a word to describe items that you don't have to buy but choose to. *Discretionary* can also describe the money you use to buy such items.

FOOD SHELF: a charity that collects food donations and distributes them to low-income people

HOSPICE: a service that provides care for people who are dying and comfort for their families

LANDFILL: an area where garbage is dumped and covered with earth

LOBBY: to attempt to convince a lawmaker to support a particular cause or vote a certain way on a bill

PETITION: a written request, often signed by many people, demanding a specific action from an authority or a government

SERVICE LEARNING: a classroom, school, or group activity that mixes classroom learning with hands-on community service

SELECTED BIBLIOGRAPHY

Corporation for National and Community Service. *Building Active Citizens: The Role of Social Institutions in Teen Volunteering*. Brief 1 in the Youth Helping America series. Washington, DC, November 2005.

———. *Building Active Citizens: The Role of Social Institutions in Teen Volunteering*. Youth Helping America series. November 2005. http://www.worldvolunteerweb.org/fileadmin/docdb/pdf/2006/05_1130_LSA_YHA_study.pdf (November 9, 2011).

———. *College Students Helping America*. October 2006. http://www.nationalservice.gov/pdf/06_1016_RPD_college_full.pdf (November 9, 2011).

———. *Educating for Active Citizens: Service-Learning, School-Based Service, and Youth Civic Engagement*. Youth Helping America series. March 2006. http://www.nationalservice.gov/pdf/06_0323_SL_briefing_factsheet.pdf (November 9, 2011).

———. *Volunteering in America*. August 9, 2011. http://www.volunteeringinamerica.gov/index.cfm (November 9, 2011).

Farber, Katy. *Change the World with Service Learning: How to Create, Lead, and Assess Service Learning Projects*. Lanham, MD: Rowman and Littlefield Publishers, 2011.

Hanc, John. "Young Activists Practice Their Pitches for Nonprofits." *New York Times,* November 10, 2010. http://www.nytimes.com/2010/11/11/giving/11CAMP .html?scp=10&sq=volunteer%20teens&st=cse (November 9, 2011).

Shaw, Randy. *The Activist's Handbook*. Los Angeles: University of California Press, 2001.

Yes Kidz Can! "Research on Volunteerism." 2011. http://www.yeskidzcan.com/research.html (November 9, 2011).

FURTHER INFORMATION

Ahlpin, Mikki. *It's Your World—If You Don't Like It, Change It: Activism for Teenagers.* New York: Simon Press, 2004.
Learn more about what it takes to be a teen activist. This title is packed full of stories of real teens finding success as activists.

American Red Cross: Volunteer
http://www.redcross.org/en/volunteer
The Red Cross helps people recover from all sorts of disasters. Check out this site to learn more about volunteer opportunities with the Red Cross.

Donovan, Sandy. *Communication Smarts: How to Express Yourself Best in Conversations, Texts, E-mails, and More.* Minneapolis: Twenty-First Century Books, 2013.
Brush up on your speaking, writing, and online communication skills—all of which you can put to work as a volunteer or an activist.

Do Something
http://www.dosomething.org
Check out this site for news, event announcements, and a searchable list of volunteer opportunities.

Edge, Laura B. *We Stand as One: The International Ladies Garment Workers Strike, New York, 1909.* Minneapolis: Twenty-First Century Books, 2011.
This title takes you behind the scenes as female workers became activists in a famous 1909 strike.

Gralla, Preston. *Complete Idiot's Guide to Volunteering for Teens.* Royersford, PA: Alpha Publishing, 2001.
Find tips and advice for locating volunteer opportunities, knowing what will be expected, and how to get started.

Great Nonprofits
http://greatnonprofits.org
Visit this site for information and reviews of hundreds of nonprofit organizations. Volunteers, clients, and other stakeholders submit reviews daily to this site.

Habitat for Humanity: Youth Programs
http://www.habitat.org/youthprograms
Habitat for Humanity builds homes for low-income families. The organization has volunteer opportunities for kids as young as nine. It's a great way to help out, learn about the building industry, and have some fun

Lewis, Barbara A. *The Teen Guide to Global Action.* Minneapolis: Free Spirit
Publishing, 2007.
Read about young people from more than thirty countries who have worked
for social change around the world, and get inspired about your own project.

Petronis, Lexi. *47 Things You Can Do for the Environment.* San Francisco: Zest
Books, 2012.
Read about the many small (and big) things that teens can do to make a
positive difference for the environment.

The Service Learning Youth Site: For High Schoolers
http://www.servicelearning.org/youthsite/high-school
Learn more about service learning, read about the actions of "Service-
Learning VIPs," and search and share ideas for projects at your school.

United Way
http://liveunited.org
This nationwide organization provides volunteers and activists for
thousands of charitable groups around the country. Check out its home
page for information on volunteering and activism.

Waldman, Jackie. *Teens with the Courage to Give: Young People Who Triumphed
over Tragedy and Volunteered to Make a Difference.* Newburyport, MA:
Conari Press, 2000.
Read about the real-life experiences of thirty teens who overcame their own
challenges and found a way to volunteer to make a difference for others.

Youth Activism Project
http://youthactivismproject.org
This nonprofit encourages teens to speak up and find lasting solutions to
problems about which they care deeply.

Youth Volunteer Corps
http://www.yvca.org
Learn more about volunteering through this national group that places
eleven- to eighteen-year-olds in volunteer and service learning opportunities.

INDEX

ABOUT THE AUTHOR

Sandy Donovan has written many books for teens, including *Communication Smarts: How to Express Yourself Best in Conversations, Texts, E-mails, and More* in the USA Today Teen Wise Guides series. She has a bachelor's degree in journalism and political science and a master's degree in public policy. She lives in Minneapolis with her husband, two sons, and a dog named Fred.